COMMAND LINE

OPERATE YOUR COMPUTER VIA
THE COMMAND PROMPT

MOMOH S.O

CONTENTS

PREFACE

Both basic and advanced operations on PCs,Computers can be carried out using the command prompt Functionality.
A mastery of the command Lines and codes helps to simplify and make operations Seamless around the computer.
This book shows the various command lines and their functions.

Thereby setting the foundation for command prompt operations.
Access the computer and carry out

operations around the computer using the computer command prompt.

ABOUT THE AUTHOR

The Author,Momoh S.O
is well-read programmer,
developer & analyst
with a B.sc in Computer
Engineering & technology.
The Author has an advanced
knowledge in the field of
engineering and web app
development & coding.
He is vast in a number of
programming language
Such as;Php,Javascript
& also HTML &
CSS.

SUMMARY

Both basic and advanced operations on PCs,Computers can be carried out using the command prompt Functionality.
A mastery of the command Lines and codes helps to simplify and make operations Seamless around the computer.
This book shows the various command lines and their functions. Thereby setting the foundation for command prompt operations.

INTRODUCTION

Users of windows command Prompt are usually perceived as advanced analysts which is not far from the truth. However knowing some of these lines and how to apply them can put you in their league.

 sWith the command lines Operations become seamless. This books looks at basic Operations from turning off, Restarting,logging off and Aborting these tasks to moderate operations such as partitioning & disk/drive checks,connecting computers,task scheduling & reminder/alarm settings, opening of hidden contents and files and more.

USING THE COMMAND PROMPT

To carry out operations via the prompt we need to install the DOS command software or application orit's equivalent on the computer.

The dos command prompt usually come Preinstalled in all versions of Windows operating system. To use the command prompt, We have to;

>Launch the command prompt

In windows;Go to

Hit the windows button
and type
Command or cmd to display
Prompt.

>**Click on the command prompt**
It opens as;

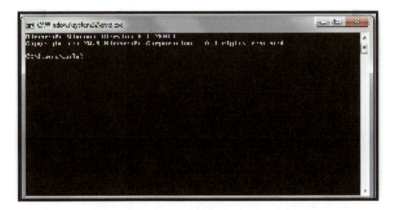

A console for decoding command lines

>**Type in the command lines or Codes.Then hit ENTER**

In the above the command line
'HELP' Which gives the above.
Output above when we hit
enter button.
Use the same procedure for
All other code lines

COMMAND LINES

Different command generates or execute different instruction. Some command prompt operations include;

Shutdown the computer

To shutdown the

computer via
The command prompt,type;
>Shutdown/s
In to the prompt console
This gives;

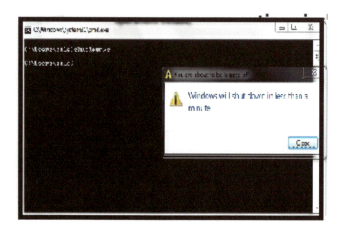

A pop up message saying 'windows will close in less than a minute'

To query for other related Or more operations,

>Type shutdown/?
This gives;

This gives a list of other related command lines

-To shutdown & restart the computer,
>Type;Shutdown/r

-TO SHUTDOWN & RESTART THE

Computer. After system is rebooted,
>**Type**;Shutdown/g

-TO HIBERNATE COMPUTER;

>**Type**;Shutdown/h

-To for running program to close,

>**Type**;Shutdown/f

--To set time-out period before

- TO SCHEDULE A TASK,OPEN

DEVICE MANAGER,STORAGE, SERVICES & APPLICATIONS ETC.

>**Type;**compmgmt.msc

This gives;

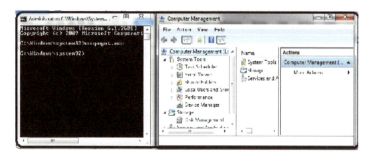

A computer management console opens.

-TO GET A COMPUTER'S INFO AND
SPECIFICATIONS...

>**Type;** Systeminfo **the hit enter**

This Gives;

This gives the entire system Information plus specifications

-TO SET UP OR ACCESS NETWORK CONNECTION CENTER

>Type;ncpa.cpl then hit enter.

This gives;

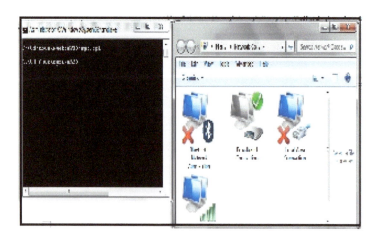

SHUTDOWN
>**Type**;Shutdown/t

**--To turn-off local computer
Without warning or time-out**
>**Type**;Shutdown/p

--To log-off local computer
>**Type**;Shutdown/l

**-- To display the graphical
User interface**
>**Type**;Shutdown/i

**-- To ABORT or INTERRUPT
A shutdown**

> Type;**Shutdown/a**

-- To document the reason for shutdown

>Type;**Shutdown/d**

- TO OPEN INSTALLED APPS & SOFTWARES

>Type;appwiz.cpl

This gives;

A List of installed software

**on the computer that can
be uninstalled.**

ACCESSING NETWORKS

-TO OPEN RESOURCE MONITOR

>Type;resmon then hit
Enter button

This gives;

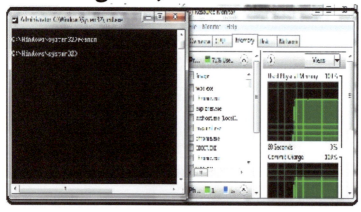

-TO MANAGE & MAINTAIN DISK & COMPUTER DRIVES

>Type;Chkdsk then hit
Enter button
   RESULT
This RUNS a diagnostic
Check on the disk for;
Errors,disk space,bad files etc

>CHKDSK/F helps to fix
Bad disk sector

>USE;Chkdsk/? for more
Options

OTHER COMMAND LINES INCLUDE;

Accessibility Controls – zaccess.cpl

Accessibility Wizard – accwiz

Add Hardware Wizard – hdwwiz.cpl

Add/Remove Programs – appwiz.cpl

Administrative Tools – control admintools

Automatic Updates – wuaucpl.cpl

Bluetooth Transfer Wizard – fsquirt

Calculator – calc

Certificate Manager – certmgr.msc

Character Map – charmap

Check Disk Utility – chkdsk

Clipboard Viewer – clipbrd

Command Prompt – cmd

Component Services – dcomcnfg

Computer Management
– compmgmt.msc

Control Panel – control

Date and Time Properties
– timedate.cpl

DDE Shares – ddeshare

Device Manager – devmgmt.msc

Direct X Troubleshooter – dxdiag

Disk Cleanup Utility – cleanmgr

Disk Defragment – dfrg.msc

Disk Management – diskmgmt.msc

Disk Partition Manager – diskpart

Display Properties – control desktop

Display Properties – desk.cpl

Troubleshooting Utility – drwtsn32

. Driver Verifier Utility – verifier

Event Viewer – eventvwr.msc

Files and Settings Transfer Tool – migwiz

File Signature Verification Tool – sigverif

Findfast – findfast.cpl

Firefox – firefox

Folders Properties – control folders

Fonts – control fonts

Fonts Folder – fonts

Free Cell Card Game – freecell

Game Controllers – joy.cpl

Group Policy Editor) – gpedit.msc

Hearts Card Game – mshearts

. Help and Support – helpctr

HyperTerminal – hypertrm

Iexpress Wizard – iexpress

Indexing Service – ciadv.msc

. Internet Connection Wizard – icwconn1

Internet Explorer – iexplore

Internet Properties – inetcpl.cpl

Keyboard Properties – control keyboard

Local Security Settings – secpol.msc

Local Users and Groups – lusrmgr.msc

Logs You Out Of Windows – logoff

Malicious Software Removal Tool – mrt

Microsoft Chat – winchat

Microsoft Movie Maker – moviemk

Microsoft Paint – mspaint

Microsoft Syncronization Tool – mobsync

Minesweeper Game – winmine

Mouse Properties – control mouse

Mouse Properties – main.cpl

Netmeeting – conf

Net Connections – control netconnections

Network Connections – ncpa.cpl

Network Setup Wizard – netsetup.cpl

Notepad – notepad

Object Packager – packager

Data Source Administrator – odbccp32.cpl

On Screen Keyboard – osk

Outlook Express – msimn

Paint – pbrush

Password Properties – password.cpl

Performance Monitor – perfmon.msc

Performance Monitor – perfmon

Phone and Modem Options – telephon.cpl

Phone Dialer – dialer

Pinball Game – pinball

Power Configuration
– powercfg.cpl

Printers and Faxes –
control printers

Printers Folder – printers

Regional Settings – intl.cpl

Registry Editor – regedit

. Registry Editor – regedit32

Remote Access Phonebook
– rasphone

Remote Desktop – mstsc

Removable Storage
– ntmsmgr.msc

RemovableStorage –
ntmsoprq.msc

Resultant Set of Policy – rsop.msc

Scanners and Cameras – sticpl.cpl

Scheduled Tasks –
control schedtasks

Security Center – wscui.cpl

Services – services.msc

Shared Folders – fsmgmt.msc

Shuts Down Windows – shutdown

Sounds and Audio – mmsys.cpl

Spidee Card Game – spider

SQL Client Configuration – cliconfg

**System Configuration
Editor –** sysedit

**System Configuration
Utility –** msconfig

System Information – msinfo32

System Properties – sysdm.cpl

Task Manager – taskmgr

TCP Tester – tcptest

Telnet Client – telnet

**User Account Management
–** nusrmgr.cpl

Utility Manager – utilman

Windows Address Book – wab

Windows Address Book – wabmig

Windows Explorer – explorer.

Boot Configuration Data - bcdedit

Editing Boot Settings - bootcfg

Encrypting or Decrypting Files - cipher

Clearing the screen - cls

usernames/passwords - cmdkey

Changing CMD Color - color

Compressing files - compress

Converting FAT drives to NTFS - convert

Delete files - del

Deleting User Profiles - delprof

Displaying the list of files - dir

Displaying Message On Screen - echo

Deleting one or more files - erase

Opening the windows Explorer - explorer

. Formatting a disk - format

Knowing file extension - ftype

Displaying the Mac Address - getmac

Online help - help

Displaying the host name - hostname

Editing disc label - label

Log a user off - logoff

. Get a log time in a file - logtime

Creating .cab files - makecab

Creating new folders- md

Opening Windows Installer - msiexec

Managing the network resources - net

Knowing the permissions for a user - perms

Testing a network connecting - ping

Printing a text file - print

Shutdown computer - psshutdown

Checking free disk space - freedisk

Know the file and volume
utilities - fsutil

File transfer protocl - ftp

Showing the space used - diskuse

Deleting a folder/ all
subfolders - deltree

Importing or Exporting
data - csvde

Policy information - gpresult
Group policy settings - gpupdate

Comparing two files - fc

Finding a text string in a file - find

Finding for a strings in file - findstr

Displaying the memory
usage - mem

Remote desktop protocol - mstsc

Managing the domain - netdom

Manage the Background-
bitsadmin

Break Capability in CMD - break

Change the permissions
of files - cacls

Call batch - call

certification services - certutil

Change a folder - cd

NTFS file system - chkntfs

Copy other location - copy

show the mapping- coreinfo

Import/Export data - csvde

Display the date
or change it - date

Display disk usage - diruse
View used space in
folder - diskuse

list of device drivers
- driverquery

View objects in active directory - dsget

Modify objectse directory - dsmod

Display the print queue status - lpq

Display open files - open files

Monitor performanc - perfmon

Access service status - rasdial

Managing RAS connections - rasphone

Send A Message - msg

Create a symbolic Link - mklink

Send email - mapisend

monitor logs - logman

Uncompressfiles - expand

Loop command - for

Move anObject - dsmove

Active directory - dsget

Active directory ACLs - DSACLs

r offline files - CSCcmd

Windows event log - sysmon

Edit file permissions - subinacl

Save and chang directory - pushd

Display user session - quser

Read - reg registry

Register - regsvr32

Batch process multiple files - forfiles

Search for Items - dsquery

Cleanup temp file, recycle bin - cleanmgr

To close prompt window-Exit

Compare the contents files - comp

map between processors - coreinfo

Manage RAS connections - rasdial

kill process by process and name id - pskill

Disconnect desktop session - tsdiscon

Edit the service principal name - setspn

Share a folder or printer- rmtshare

Change the registry permissions - regini

>To get more info about a command line-
Use;
Command name/?
Also type HELP into the prompt

-To connect two computers A be able able to exchange View content

>Type;mstsc
Then hit ENTER
Output: a dialog box

Asking for computer 2 Name,hit ENTER & Connect.

CONCLUSION

At the of this book it is expected that a rookie or novice with no prior knowledge of the command lines and use of command prompt to have a well laid foundation the use of command prompt to various tasks and operations.

It serves as a manual to analyzing computer structure and function.

START LEARNING

& PRACTICE NOW !

Do Leave a rating on the book page in the kindle store!

COMPUTER TECHNOLOGY MASTERY

In a fast paced and advancing digital world where the use of computers have become a

common place and order of the day.

From free-lancing,online gigs, such as proof-reading & editing,coding,graphic design,video editing,

scripting,web design,spreadsheet & gaming as well as it's use in the corporate world .

Computer hot key mastery and coding skills are essential and near compulsory if we ever want to be efficient and move

speedily & efficiently working with PCs and our computers.

This series contain books to help you learn different computer technological operation s like web design,coding use of command prompt and keyboard mastery to help users level up their computer skill and use the

computer seamlessly.

Color Codes

The importance of Color cannot be Over-emphasized from the addition of color to fonts,

margins,backgrounds and Other web page elements to It's use graphic arts,paintings

and more.

This book COLOR CODES contains various colors & their codes to help ease

the incorporation of colors in web design & other areas applicable.Thereby removing

the stress of having to refer to a given color.Color code is a manual for learners and
Professionals alike.
For Web designers & Developers,Soft ware & App developers,Graphic Artists and designers and so on.

Computer Hot Key Mastery: Operate The Computer Seamlessly

In a fast advancing digital world where the use of computers have become a
common place and order of the day.
From free-lancing,online gigs, such as proof-reading & editing,coding,graphic design,video editing,
scripting,web design,spreadsheet & gaming as well as it's use in the corporate world .
Computer hot keys are essential and near compulsory if we ever want to be efficient and move
speedily & efficiently working with PCs and our computers.
This book lists some hot keys or keyboard shortcuts that facilitate and make the operationof the
computer seamless.

Html A-Z: All Operations In Html

HTML isthe language of the web, it is the frame-work of the web and website development.It is to a website what the skeleton is to the human body.
HTML A-Z is the ultimate book for html,as it simplifies,summarizes and explains all the integral aspects and components with practical examples,illustrations and application of HTML codes.
The book contains practical examples and illustrations to help learners and developers of all levels from beginner or rookie,students,intermediate to seasoned professionals to

understand the language at a glance.

It delves in to the basics and core advanced topics from placing of text on a web page,to listing of items,addition of colors,forms;like text boxes,password box,drop-down lists,clickable buttons,Option or radio button,submit button,search ,to box query,addition of images to page,links, navigation page links,addition of clickable images to link objects,replacing links with graphic objects and other media files. Addition of downloadable contents such as;pdf,docx files,media files such as images,videos,animations,etc.